To Debbie
In Loving Fr...
(These are my ...
Francie's) ...

Candle Fire Seen Through a Honey Jar

by

Frances Heiman

authorHOUSE™

1663 LIBERTY DRIVE, SUITE 200
BLOOMINGTON, INDIANA 47403
(800) 839-8640
WWW.AUTHORHOUSE.COM

First published by AuthorHouse 09/27/04

ISBN: 1-4184-9341-4 (sc)

Printed in the United States of America
Bloomington, Indiana

This book is printed on acid-free paper.

For Rachel
In memory

Gold

A gold mosaic of Autumn leaves
Adorns the city street;
wreathes of smoke rise
through the Indian Summer haze.
Sun spangles on the river
mingle with sculptured clouds.
A thread of gold runs through this day.
And in the country fields
gold lemon lilies flaunt
the porcelain frost that clothes the grass.
Earth sighs and pleads to an ancient wind.
Gold grains lie among
the whispery rows of corn.
The trees are a rich brocade
of tapestry against the sky.
There are fingers that press the fields
and rub the shine of finitude,
birds that weave in flocks
like moving stars.
At sunset, bare boughs, black filigree
are etched against a rose gold sky.
Gold lantern moon
rises through layers of dark and white.
Gold eye of a rabbit
hiding under the pines.
In the darkness
no one hears
the silken feet of creatures in the woods.
Even the silence praises God.
In our frail being is our hope
of living to love.
Jesus the Lover of all
Love gave You the gifts
of gold and frankincense and myrrh.
You gave us the gift of wine
to drink of this moment
in such a gold grail.

Gift for a Grown Daughter

Never could pearls cover you
or fire adorn the flame within,
silk from the finest thread would tear;
The bloodstone, garnet bare themselves
as brittle shields;
nor could some golden apple on a chain
or silver amulets conceal
how light along the road
is cupped in fragile glass;
no lace or satin could reveal
how spattered stains of leaves
on full moon night
swim through the whispering grass.
I covered your small bones
with fingers like a fern
or spider silk
that shelters hummingbirds, my touch.
Now you are painted by wind
and spangled by the pageantry of roads
which bless and wound.
I plead some shelter for a grown child.
Words are the only precious stones I wear
my sanctuary for the night,
your story, mine,
the praise of flesh and bone
of leaf and bough
since the first time
that hand touched hand
or hearts could love and grieve.
Words are the shimmering gems
gathered from antiquity
words shouted across the silent prairie;
words, the seed for the heart's bread,
your sacred scroll and mine,
symbols read or sung
to mend the tattered laurels of goldleaf
We place upon our heads
when we are young.

Silk Screen

Carved quiet morning,
the gray mist a skein
clothing trees and hills.
The black November fields
are interlaced with Winter wheat.
Prairie stems stand sculptured still;
stacks of hay, bread loaves for a giant,
rest in the silence, brush stroked, eloquent.
Lace boughs are delicate upon the glazed sky,
their bold calligraphy
muted into soft, dark hills.
A swift embroidery of birds
glean the last corn.
Underneath the fog enameled woods
the eyes of little foxes,
bird nests bound with spider silk...
Three deer leap out of the haze
and stop by the road,
their eyes brown emblems
polished from a journey
through the intangible boughs,
their wild stare sealed
upon the muted apparitions of hills;
they plunge again
into the morning's silk.

My Father's Hands

moved among the peonies
heavy with ivory and fuchsia blooms
on a hot day in August;
flies stuck to my legs,
wind breathed through the trees
shivering the leaves
of the Tree of Heaven
by his bedroom window.
His long, thin fingers
wove the brilliant roses;
picked a perfect rose
yellow with tinges of pink
my mother's favorite
the Peace Rose.
My brother and I
stood barefoot
on the cold linoleum floor
while he went to cut the switch.
His hair hung over his eyes
while he lashed some old enemy
beat the mother who beat his spirit away
while they lived in abandoned railroad cars
when their shack on the Green River flooded.
After the whipping
he looked calm;
went out into the dark at night
among the roses
and smoked his pipe,
while roaches ran in lines
over our beds.
I read my copy of Grimm's
and slept in the soft darkness
dreamed of the place in Indiana
where I saw the footprint
of the angel Gabriel.

Cat O'Nine Tail Song

My father carved me with a whip
the branch with its searing whine
played on my ribs and bones
licked the quivering skin away.
His fingers were old parchment
stained from the past
He wrote his grief on my skin.
I came howling into the world
wrapped in my grandmother's whispers.
Like old sepia photographs
she lived in another time
shrouded in the smoke of Vicksburg
where her father died.
The old rage
is an antique handed down
one generation to another.
I was swallowed in the belly
of my smallness
my bones stamped
like a fossil print on rock.
Now my children
stand in the smoke and shadows
bear too
the imprint of my smallness
bear the burden of darkness
born in the scent and death of Vicksburg.
They hold centuries
in their frail bones.

Waiting for Robyn

My grandchild sleeps
in a jeweled sea;
blossoms in blood bright fields
this secret child that grows
beneath my daughter's ribs
her bones carved ivory
her blue black eyes obsidian.
She has wrinkled feet
like an old woman's
and waits for the first hungry breath
close to the beat
of her mother's heart
her own heart
like a drum
beats in its perfect time
reliable as ocean waves.
The coils of her brain
embroidered with bones,
she sucks her thumb, they say
her skin dazzling
while she dances and kicks
in this sea where her life began.
My child and her child
walk through centuries
of stars and planets and clouds
while they wait for this bloom
to unfold
hands waiting to clap
voice set for singing
little seed in its pod
pearl in s shell.
Now that I am an old woman
I pray for this child
who sleeps in rhythm with stars.
I wait to tell her about the world.

A King's Daughter

I was his treasure
his fair rose, he said,
when we walked the Summer meadows
hand in hand;
or he, on his shoulders, carried me,
a princess through a radiant land
where the flowers grew wild and bold
and flocks sang swimming
through the sun's hot gold.
Then something happened to this man.
He did not laugh
or lead me through the blooming woodlands,
hiding, he counted pearls, cupped coins
beneath cool fists.
And then one day I ran to hold
the one I loved the most.
I thought he must have been afraid of growing old.
He touched me with his shimmering hands
and I leaped out of childhood into gold.

Festival

When the Winter sky burns rose
and the Christ Child is coming
when darkness weaves a mask around windows
where the fire mingles with frost
and children trace the stars;
when the Wise Men's steps
crackle over the frozen brush,
when even the fires have died
and embers bloom in the dark;
when all the voices of the earth
are gathered into song
and angels dwell in the deep quiet,
their hands peeling the petals of night
down to its gold, and the stars form
one field of light
around a holy place
and the midnight wind
gathers the trees to prayer
then do not even whisper
for the Child is near.

The Mask of Agamemnon

The golden mask that gilds his bones
for centuries was buried in the dust,
the mask of one who sacrificed his child
then died from his wife's hate.
These ruins whistle a sad song
a golden flute whose ancient tones
rise from the dark, and he uncovered,
mask aside, would be a skull
and if his daughter's ghost rose from the dark
would she pluck this wild flower
leaving skull and mask
letting the past lie in its memories of blood?
Or would she wander through the ruined city
crying, I was killed for gold
for wind to sail the foaming sea
for silver goblets, golden leaves
engraved with butterflies.
My flesh and bones were sacrificed
for that mortality he feared.
He took my life to build a world
lost now among the winds, the wild blooms
that spring forever from this wilderness.

Pharaoh's Daughter

Listen to me now, my dearest friend
stay with me while I watch the ark.
I asked my daughter
to stand among the river reeds.
When Amran comes in from the fields
you will be the one to tell him
his son lives, or comfort him.
We both may die
if this plan fails.
Then you must tell him why
I took a basket, sealed it tight
with clay and tar
and placed our child in it.
Three months have passed
since that sweet bitter day when he was born.
I can no longer bear his cradle songs to be
the stamp of Pharaoh's soldiers
night falling,
listening for every creak,
jumping at the night owl's call.
If I can only shelter one small life
from Pharaoh's law....

I have watched each day
while Pharaoh's laughing girl
a favorite of her father, some say,
sheds her linen gowns to dance in water,
this young and gentle woman
who will not watch the waters
cleared of snakes and crocodiles.
She bends to touch a battered dragonfly
and cups her hands around some fledgling
fallen from its nest.
There is a longing born in all, I think
that begs for something small
and if she wants my son to play
then she will hide him in her father's court
carry him perched upon her shoulder
like some bright young bird that's wounded.

She's coming now!
The slave girl wades the water
brings him to the princess.
Now she holds my boy up in the air
her laughing face up to the sun
then sits, cross -legged on the sand
now looks as if she is in prayer.
My daughter walks to them
watches the princess and her toy.
They're calling me and I must go.
Tell Amran I will sing him cradle songs
of Yahweh, whisper to him Israel.

A Mother's Elegy

for Chris)

Crack of the door
click of the latch
he was running when I saw him last,
weaving through the wild rye fields
my grown boy, floating away
like a seed on a silvery milkweed.

He sang his songs of Summer
but mourned the broken creatures
found on his path,
the rabbit shrieking in the night,
the wing bent sparrow left to die,
the dance of the web caught fly.

Now I am not a patriarch
and cannot rage
like Jacob for his son,
nor can I understand
this boy's sleep

in such a field of roses.
I have stunned my mind
to keep it safe
and sit here in my dark dress
my mind like a wheel
turning above a shallow creek.

Crack of the hatchet
click of the blade
beat of the thresher's wheel;
eye of the lens that flashes quick
you caught my boy with golden hair
while he ran through forever fields.

Imprint

What music, art, what words
can match your touch upon their skin?
Your eyes engraved their bones.
They flutter moth like from a covering
thin as a scroll.
Your wrote upon parchment
when your fingers
sang them to a gentle sleep.
What gold engravings from an ancient ruin
or marbled flesh carved to form
can match the imprint of your touch
upon their mottled infant skin
upon the brittle bones
you covered with your heart's cloth
and marked a rubric on their palms and feet.
It is like leaves etched on rocks
or wings caught in amber centuries ago,
ancient imprints of a symbol
stamped on clay or wax
the eloquent mosaic in your mind
artist with an etching needle
printing on fine glass
your imprint now an heirloom.
For generations they will bear
all you have chiseled on them
with something soft as rain.
Their children will not know they sing
because the music in you
brushed indelibly upon your child.

Abandoned House

Whoever builds a shelter
for the heart
builds laughter
song, a place for bread,
hearth for the fire, the making of lace.
The place that shelters human flesh
is a place of prayer
the light sweet wine of love
pressed to the lips or spilled.

The old house sighs and will not stop living.
It holds memories like pressed flowers in a book.
They spill out, sepia colored
to grace the battered frame.
There were hands working
holding new life
in these rooms,
children's bare feet
whispered against old floors.
It was a place for crying
the cradle's rhythmic rock,
bread rising, sun splashing
the walls, and a hot wind.
The roof caught snow,
rain polished the wood.
Did someone light candles.
hang a bright plate on the wall
listen to the song of wild geese?
A seed splits its husk to die in birth,
the rose spills out its heart in petals.
The old house sleeps under a few stars,
trembles awake and listens at night.

Elegy for an Amish Child

(This poem was written after reading about an
Amish child killed when someone threw a rock
at the family as they were traveling in their
buggy.)

You crossed an ancient path,
porcelain martyr,
little girl with white cap, gray gown,
one of the plain people
who sought a new land
refused to carry arms or war..
They made you an anchorite,
hidden among the songs of the field
where blooms blow
from the breath of an old prairie.

Does your mother watch above you
hold her hollowed arms in prayer
weep for your journey
you the laughing vagabond
crossing sacred waters in your flimsy ark?
You could have clapped your hands that day

Bathed in the childworld
Your laughter breaking like buds
Upon the silent road
Until you slept and your horse,
pale, apocalyptic, pulled you to fire
the carriage shimmering with lanterns
weaving through the mesh of the night.
Sweet cradled crucifix
You have born the blind dark's blow
you the fallen lark
lying among the whispered prints of Indians
who once leaped the unbroken land.
All those who gather around this flaming field
would bless you in the hushed grave
and bless the fragile hands
that flung you to this dark,

the blind, now grieving eyes
that bear the memory of your death.
Bright lantern with translucent skin
candle held to the wind,
forgive us in our shelters of shattered bone,
who carve our wounds upon the world
forgive the creeds turned into stone.
forgive the cracked cathedral thrown,
it's stained glass bleeds on the earth;
pardon the faith that shelters only its own,
Peace lies in the bright mosaic eyes
of those who gather the world into their gaze.
Quick winnowed child
shielded in the holy deep
forgive the weapons and the words
that stoned you to this smiling sleep.

Candle fire Seen Through a Honey Jar

Van Gogh painted fields
the color of this fire.
John the Baptist could have gazed
on flaming honey
lit by the desert sun.
Fire caught in glazed glass
splinters into shapes,
a luminous patch in the sky-
the nebulae.
Or this small field
becomes the tongues of lilies
flicking pollen to the wind,
or a harvest moon
through frosted glass,
the slight flame's cosmic blaze
spun to a chain of gold.
West Indies lanterns held fireflies
and in some ancient place
the oily carcasses of animals
were strung with wicks
wild lanterns against the raven sky.
Once fire was sacred, tended
carried by nomads guarding coals.
Their hollowed stones held gold light.
The sun becomes a candle
through stained glass
and carves the windows of cathedrals.

I watch my honey jar, my lantern
with the candle beside it
bloom from the seeds of ancient fires.
The flame is the heart
the glass its ribs and bones
honey for oil, the moment a wick
that flames to catch the vision of the universe
in bits of amber glass.
Is the honey splintered into stars a vigil light
quiet, small among the walls of dark
where the Winter winds sting with sleet
and the trees shake in their naked sleep
and there are whispers of holocaust?

17

Frances Heiman

Country Gravestones

Sparrows grace the field of stones
chiseled by rain
where Queen Anne's lace
like sea foam rises
over the wild rye grain;
locusts chant requiems;
rain drums on Silver Poplars,
glazes prairies blades
that stand bronze and still.
In Autumn the wild rose peels and breaks.
Here the quiet moth-like around the sight
of stone worn smooth as a fingered bead;
a mother and four infants
their scrolls left among the crimson brush.

They were un-named
gathered around her as for cradle songs
or like stars in a constellation
their porcelain bones,
strings of pearls undone.
She must have sung to the storm
carried their flesh like candle fire.
She knew the sacrifice of breath and bone
the first marked by cries
the last with stone.

Now a million scarlet voices
speak from the hills;
trees bleed gold and red to the earth.
Soon snow will cover the burnished scripts.
hiding the steadfast sacrifice
until Spring rains reveal the rosary again.

"The wolf is now my brother, owls of the desert have become my companions . Job 30

My Brother, the Wolf

Every year he takes more of me
my heart a bitten half-moon he feeds upon,
licking the quiet trickling of life.
He comes often now,
wild brother with a primeval stare,
his paw prints delicate in snow.
He breathes hot on my spine.
His tongue carves a hovel for my mind.
I am easily caught and torn now.
He makes stains on me
when we wrestle together in our rock crevice
where I hide from the blistering footprints of God.
I wear his baby teeth as a necklace
and when he sleeps I finger the milk soft bones
like a prayer or an amulet,
knowing he has grown in my mind.
He has always stood nearby,
but I have never before
felt the thump of his heart,
or the heat of his jaw.
There is such stealth in death,
the hunter killing before the Fall moon,
the snapping trap in the silent dark.
I see his tracks and wait.

Nightsong to a Firstborn

Unguarded child, you the sacrifice
held lamblike by your spindly feet,
washed now from a sticky birth veil
and wrapped in lace, you sleep
and do not hear the beat
of strange horsemen
treading your stainless cells.
You are christened in the night
while your eyes are closed
imprinted by ancestors
who chisel their shadows
on your yielding head.
Your eyes bear the scars
of your grandfathers' knives
some angel barely stopped.
Your cradle songs are played
from ancient pipes
old songs of your fathers
who died at Vicksburg
or fled the Holocaust.
Their wounds swathe your heart.
Silhouettes of dark horsemen
interlace your bones.
You should have fiery angels
like those who guarded Eden
hover above your hushed crib
letting you dangle
your wrinkled feet in paradise
you like the first seal on the universe.

Mary's Psalm

For flesh and bones
my child will rest
in a web of stars;
night winds whine
and creatures with eyes
like coals of fire
rise from sleep
to tell the magic of these woods,
the stillness of the Cedars
and the wild fields sing
the story of my love.
My lover has come down to this garden
To walk in the beds of spice.

I exult, housing God
like Hannah
sing of the spangled world
imprinted with the flesh of God,
tell of the bread for the hungry child,
paschal light for the prisoner.
I cannot sing of Pharaoh drowning
or armies in a siege,
my child will not break
a bruised reed
but wear the scaffold of his gentleness.
My lover has come down to this garden,
He gathers the lilies now.

This moment is engraved
on the world,
the day a bloom of fire on the dark,
gold the wind
even the shadows gold,
branches of grapes
tremble on the vine.
My house of petals
bears no thorns.
I weave blooms
into many colored coats

21

for the desolate.
Sing praise!
He has filled the hungry with good things.
My son leaps
at the gaunt child's cry.
I will seek him
whom my heart loves.

Cat's Cradle

There is no amniotic grace,
your birth a cold, wet pain
slithering placenta, bloodstained, stark...
moments after birth the newborn kitten stood
wet and wailing
blind and begging
slicked down seal face lifted up
in search, and the cry
the startling old cry
that shouts "I will be."
There is only the cold damp birth
life all tied together with a string
little thin umbilical
separating breath and the dark.

Your mother runs at first in fear
then licks away those waters
where you swam, unknowing, dark and safe.
Later the furry cuddling
the dry warm breath of birth
and opening of eyes.
Later you and your sister
will stalk shadow mice
upon the window sill
and wander through star spilling fields
to search a sleeping bird.

Will your mother fear
your tight-rope journey,
your silent catpaw walk
through sweet dark places
threaded by the night's shining nets?

String cradles for her kittens
rocked now in the velvet of tongue and fur,
and then the wandering
the quivering hairline stroll through dark.

23

My Grandmother's Eyes

...became like blackened chimney lamps,
glass stained with soot,
holding a small flame
they fed on dark fields in her mind.
She, the young widow
sat on the porch at night
singing hymns, whispered notes
dropped like petals
around the shack
by the Green River, in Kentucky.
She stared as clouds and stars
bloomed on the black water at night,
sang quavery songs
until the sun, a kettle of fire
poured its scarlet on the stream.

She wore dark dresses, black
with yellowed lace at the neck.
Seven children clung to her
their hollow eyes
like thorns upon her skin,
their nakedness to the wind
like a cloth of stone
wrapped around her flimsy bones.

"One Summer," my father said,
"She fed us mostly cabbage
and when it rained
and the shack flooded
we stayed in old railroad cars."

She would stand outside at night
look for a moon, while they slept
her face a porcelain glaze of rain,
her eyes stained from the dark
she saw descending over and over again.

"It was not always so" she murmured
in the dark of the railroad car.

24

A kiss for my daddy when I was three
and then he was gone to Vicksburg.
And when I was growed, I met Robert.
We eloped to Corydon.
I wore a yellow dress
the color of water lilies.
Babies were born and Robert rode the circuit
preaching the Word.
I thought he should plow the field on Sunday
but he wouldn't because it was the Sabbath.
And then he worked at the Locks
where he sat on the banks of the River.
And then they all was sick, Typhoid...
I nursed them all
and when he died I pressed against his face
and screamed
until I seen they was all looking at me
with eyes as big as buckets.
Will was the oldest, then Denny and Ruth.
Joey was only four, Anna a young girl
Milt the baby was two."

"We had a hard time of it
when Robert was gone.
The corn in the field
I bought with my bone.
The quilts I sewed from rags
of dresses and christening gowns.
All the morning's gold was gone.
The Dogwood blooms
from the blackest bough;
the dark fields swell with wheat;
the hunter's moon shines bright in the sky.
but me, I'm soaked with dust.
Ain't no way of threshing fields burned black.
But if I could make bread from them
I'd slice it thin
and shivering, hold it to my tongue."
She could not save them from the dark
that gathered about their eyes
clung to their hearts and bones.

25

Barefoot, they danced
upon the hot coals of her eyes.
She had some embers from the past
and tended them when the day began
the gold of the sun
cold upon a hungry child.
She whipped them with a searing branch
wild with frenzy
then she cried and prayed
tongue-tied and tired
hugged them to her stony ribs
fed them bits of bread and greens
until her sons could pay for food
by shining through the dark dawn
in their miners' hats,
until they went to war
and she could live on soldier's pay,
the seeds of Vicksburg in her heart
the green corn rising
from the ashes of another land.

Wall

Wooden cherubim guarded the walls
carved wood, washed in gold
the angels danced
above the Ark
their wings filling
the place Most Holy,
weaving in and out of time,
wild olive wings
to guard Solomon's Temple,
trumpeters chanted in the hush
in the Temple
gleaming with stones,
Bronze altar with ten gold lamps
and the bread's presence upon it.
Wild olive wings
heard pilgrim feasts
the new moons and the Sabbaths,
the shofar's cry
in the dark.
Out of the dust one bloom
this wall
bearing the heart of Solomon.
It hears prayers, whispered cries
wears stains
the gold washed from its grain
and tears shine now
fragile the parchment pleas.

Watching a Crucifix

Wind of the world's first roaring sea
Walls of Jerusalem
Chalice of pilgrims' search
Jesus, Joshua, Rabbi, Man
Turn us to thee anew.

Candles burnish the gilded pain
such fine patina shows no scars
God's golden flesh
clings, shining, to His golden bones;
this sculptured song
plucks breath to death.
We stumble and sing
to a plainchant of nail carved hands
Jesus, Joshua, Rabbi, Man
who kindles the lanterns
in our hearts-
touch, burn and fire us anew to Thee
break us to glittering,
prisoners, thieves
who clothe our brothers and sisters in ash
and turn away from the blaze
of this gold wood-
Break us to broken shimmering
turn us anew-
who touches God must touch His splendor too.

Susan

Let me die,
my ashes blow
to the four winds
I cry, abandoned by the universe,
myself in my own eyes destroyed.
Only God's Heart
can hold remorse,
bathe the blistered child in me.
I lie awake
my image twisted
through these bars.
I breathe alone.
Only the eyes of God
touch my new guise.
My father knew it too-
the night that has no light.
I long to be with him
singing in a world of stars.
He gave me the hunger for himself
that led to this waking death.
Medea mother,
even when galaxies burn
Earth will bear the stain of their blood
My sons, children of my father's child
in white they rise
while I hold their blackened bones.
Will it be forever
that I hear their cries?

Herod

There never was a person I could trust.
How I remember all the times
they told me of the children of that town
who died because of some stargazers' words,
foolish men, who left their homes
to seek an infant who would take my throne.
And there were others who would merely frown.
Then I would have them put to death
until I saw that even my own sons
would kill their father for a crown.
Miriamne turned against me too.
I had her killed so quietly one night,
my beloved, blown out like a candle
with one breath
And all the palace walls were black
and thick with faces leering down at me.
I stumbled down the halls and called
"Miriamne, Miriamne" and the sound
echoed to the vaulted roof, was lost.
I beat myself all night against those walls
and called her name
over and over again.

Letter From Emerson to His Friend Thoreau

I take to the woods each day
where scrolls of bark and fern open quietly
to hear the song of the wind
when the Jackpine trembles at dawn.
I see the world in a hidden web
my little creek part of the Sea.
You know, my friend, the moment we become
one with moss and rock and stars.
In Fall I gather the spendthrift leaves
copper and gold and plum,
the cloth of God, His many colored coat.
On a Summer morning the wild rose gleams
a goblet for the rain's old wine.
You know that God is clothed in silence
and the richest feast is solitude.
All things created bear a crack.
The one who wounds will suffer wounds.
The thief steals from himself.

Crocus Blooming

These bright fingers touch me;
sun speckles fire this yellow bloom.
It is like a woven eye of God
but nothing can unravel it.
I have never known
what makes this splendor mine
this rapture of blossoms
breaking from the earth.
God scoops up time, and sprinkles it in minutes,
in quick stabs of blooming
that cut some crevice for my eyes and mind.
I never sit beside these flowers
like a pilgrim would
but brush my hand a moment
on the day's new birth.
Spring is cracked and culled
by bright fingers.
I wait for miracles
and now, at night
a Paschal moon dangles its fire on the lawn
while some core of mine breaks open
spilling gold seeds everywhere.

Stained Glass

The prophet's pearled robe
lilies in blue and scarlet fields
the face, the eyes of Jesus
were caught in color, glass
a song, this fine mosaic with its veins of glass.
As a child
it caught me in its radiant net
Angels with their gold trumpets
played through the stillness.
Adam rose beneath a flaming tree,
Elijah's chariots were fire
sealed upon glass fields.
Underneath the shimmering wheels of prayer
and great cathedrals where pilgrims knelt
beneath the carmine glaze
of those blazing eyes of light
where glaziers of breath and bone
carved frail images of Noah, Solomon,
of David singing to his flocks
and the most bright Mother and Child
radiant in a rose of light
where children passed in fearful flight
the shimmering windows of Nuremberg
and in Toledo where the north rose window
carved the Crucifixion in bright flames
of glass and sun
and the voice of the Inquisitor
stained the earth in crimson
underneath the tapestry
of light and song, and saints
the broken martyrs bled
chained to their love they sang
and blazed in a sacred fire
their blackened bones
shutting out the sun
that carved my Eden fields.

Frances Heiman

Portrait of a Hindu Madonna

She sits on a hand woven cot
dreams of her child
her flesh shelters
the gold seed.
She wears a rose sari
blue mantle draped on the bed
her bare feet on the earthen floor
one polished drop within
her son dangling in his unborn skin.
She lives in a river of silence
No lilies, halos, no angels
only the light in her heart
lantern that glows
in her skin and bones.
An artist caught the invisible world.
Mother of God she rises perennial
through time and space.
She looks far away
could it be her anguish
over the gaunt children
that throng around her
when she walks by the river?

The image makers
gather around her fire
tell old stories
speak of angels
and how the Creator
gathered into one drop
the voice of the waters.

Glory follows the gaunt child
when the face of the earth
with its wrinkled skin
looks away.
O Mary, when you bloom on the jade sea
for mariners, you speak for the lost.
You are the young woman
who dips her feet in the river.

More knowledge than I can know.
Sometimes I cannot see
the gold painted into your eyes
If poets had not dreamed your dreams
or painters had not stood dazed
by the fire of your bright image
linked to the Mind of the universe.

Picking a Bone with Browning

I'm not downing Browning
but I am amazed to see
how such an intellect as he
could say "the best is yet to be."
And though I love his poetry
I am not clowning when I say
he must have had an off day
when he made the rabbi sage
sing glories of old age
instead of being erudite
enough to speak about the blights
and all the fights the older wage.

Browning Sir, you must have been bewitched
to preach such shibboleth
and let a kind old man speak, none the less,
who must have mourned his aching bones
in something less than dulcet tones
and thought his bursa was a curse, even worse-
old men can be crotchety
and full of animosity.
Old men can cuss
or find life dolorous.

I love your scoundrels, duchesses and counts
your fainting belles
and heroes gallant,
your frightened bishops, lovers crazed
and all those humans slightly dazed
by all the heinous labyrinths of earth-
befuddled, muddled, baffled about their worth.
But when it comes to comprehending
aging's frailty, you should not sing.
Most of your poems will attest
you really knew that love was best.
And that's the bone of my contention
Sir, it's all you do not mention.

Coals

These memories are fields of fire
my father in his last sleep
with roses on his breast
his ribs that seem to breathe again.

Now in this place of stone angels
with their stilled flight
where we brought him at last
my father travels
from dark to dark
still in his shroud of dust
like the young man
wrapped in the light of carbide lamp
digging coal for our fragile fire.

Now the last walk up the hill
pine box bobbing
over the Spring soaked mud
past dove songs, weed stalks
willows turning yellow,
the wind trembling boughs,
I sing my own silent requiem
and ask a Father for my father
Someone to wash the night away
to bear him gently to love,
A God to blow into his dusty heart
and shout "Now live."
We stand where angels
in ceramic stillness
implore the tops of trees
and listen while a train
bears a burden of coal away
even now, while these words
are poured upon the dust.
The train wails past the high grasses
meadow roses and Queen Anne's lace
wild in untouched fields
and past the shabby fronts of stores
where someone always sits in ragged silence.

37

I could not bear his silent face
or the roses placed upon him
sweet roses for this last sleep
when roses were the only thing
he nurtured into bloom.
They should have buried him
with glittering lumps of coal.
These were his heart and bones.
I do not mourn the stilled life
but the lost journey
his endless hacking at the black
his eyes were like roses
velvet longing but thorns grew from his bones.

I am engraved
by his wrathful eyes
christened like him by this dark dust,
dipped in the dark
like a candle over and over again.
I walk, stumble over his grave
in rag curls, pinafore
and high top shoes
forever dressed in smallness
standing in the soap washed fragrance
of my Sunday dress,
his eyes the blazing coals
red lantern in my heart.

Day's Eye

You bought me a print of daisies
to hang in our home;
in the late afternoon
speckles of shadow dapple the glass;
at night it catches the rose light from lamps
the leaves are the sea green
of our daughter's eyes
the petals stand quivering
in a silent wind
there is never an end to their core
gold centers tipped to the sun,
white rays, frail spokes of a prayer wheel
and at times in Winter
the birch tree outside
reflects in the glass
shadow seeds dangling
over a glass field.

Frances Heiman

A January Dusk

This twilight vigil is not one that I
would want to keep each night
like lonely widows watch the sky
its black embroidery of Winter trees,
the rose, the mauve, the streams of gray
like endless rivers run;
birds hush, blue shadows paint the snow
icicles stop their dripping in this dark
and through the kitchen window the moon
full, radiant among the ribboned clouds.
My lamp and candles bloom
lotus flowers floating on the dark,
A silence beats in the room.

Watching Jasmine Sleep

Now the snow shadowy just before dark
The trees embrace the heavens
They reach toward the twilight sky
And all is in stillness.
Now in this hour when the wind ceases
The world of black and white stands silent.
The sky turns plum color
The bare branches of trees interconnect
Like all of life.
And Jasmine sleeps
Unaware of the wheel turning on itself
Unaware of the centuries of women
Who came before her bringing life.

I hold her as the first woman held her newborn
She has taken my heart, this grand-daughter.
She sleeps under the new moon
When one bright star
Adorns the Winter sky.
Tomorrow we must teach her
About how all she touches with love
Will shelter her
Like a green canopy of leaves.
Teach her that to hurt another
Brings hurt to herself.
Compassion creates, hate destroys
And the holy is learned only with great trial.
I want the universe to watch her sleep
And all the cosmos of animals and searing stars
To keep still.
We will not awaken her, not yet.
This child lives near God's heart.

Mandala

I sat in spotless pinafore
My sandals polished
Waiting for the moving hand
Of the carousel man
Pressed to the neck
Of a satin horse
Until the pulsing whirl began
And I was carried
In the arms of the wind.
Melted to a wordless rapture
Mingled with the rhythms
Of the earth.
Such a delicate stampede
Over the breath of the night
Billowed through the blinking lights
The scent of candy apples
And popcorn in the air.
The carousel had scarlet chariots
Its ribs were poles
And music was the marrow
Spilling from its gilded bones
And when the wheel creaked to a stop
I watched the carousel man
Amazed at his face
With angry creases and eyes glazed
A deep blue tattoo on his arm
He smoked his cigarette down to the end

Then flung the fiery brand
Into the faceless night
His eyes like stone
Set in an ancient mask
How could he not be trembling
At this splendor
Guardian of a royal chariot?
I thought he was an Atlas
Bearing heaven in his hands
He thought himself a boatman
For the River Styx
And heard apocalyptic steps.

Moss Roses

Have their hearts bared
Cradle gold seeds
Blown from the breath of the Himalayas
Antique petals, china pink and velvet red
Reborn in the prairies, in the creek of
Wagon wheels.
Flowers blowing in the silent wind
Roses that prairie women gathered
Under a bark roof
They wait for the pollen scattering
Fragrant heiroglyphs
Like ancient lace or yellowed wedding gowns.
They speak of another time
I cannot catch their fire
Imprison their ever spilling hearts
They are forever blowing out of the day
Seeds crossing centuries
Rivers of golden hearts that will not stop
As if enamelled hands
Has tossed them through the radiant dark.

Outdoor theatre in Autumn

Oh my love the long light ending
And the singers
Vanished to the dark
Dancers swept away
Like leaves from Autumn boughs
But for the plover's last wild cry
Lavender voices of the lilacs
Speak of fallen petals
Through the last long night
Boatmen by the waters bending
Sow their fiery blooms of light
We rise to leave an ancient chant
Though I who have loved you would stay here
Safe in the trembling Summer leaves
Unending stay beside you
While the dancers pose
For another leap
And singers chant again
And porcelain blossoms cling to the boughs

Evensong at St. Mary's

This crucifix of polished wood
I knew as a child.
Red blooms adorn the sculptured feet
In this sanctuary where we kneel

Outside the chapel windows
The water's frozen edge
And the amazing language
Of black trees porcelain with snow.
The light of the evening sun
Threads its way through lead glass windows
And there is candlelight
Beneath the carved eyes
Compline and silence
The nuns kneel
The red blooms on the altar blaze.
All else is white, an alabaster storm
Luminous against the twilight sky.
Outside, sparrows hide from the frozen breath
Moving over the Lake
With its sheet of gray ice
Shivering in the quake of the wind.

The crimson altar should bloom
In the city's heart
In the darkness of silent streets
Scarlet blooms for the leaden eyes
Behind stained curtains.
Who will walk here
The young girls cover themselves with silk
They think they bear blooms within themselves
And do not walk with the ragged child.
Here is not the same stillness as in the woods
Where the numbed twigs whisper in the wind.
Here soliltar;y children beg alms.

Frances Heiman

In the rain of stillness
The nuns sing, their eyes enamel
Their fingers bone china
Their hands move among the pages
Like fingers plucking grain
From fields drenched in light.
In the city a spindly child on a poster stares
Now it is night
The last prayers whispered
The nuns leave quietly
The only light a red lantern
To mark the mystery in these fields.

About the Author

Frances Heiman lives in suburban Chicago and has been writing for thirty five years. She has published poetry and has won several poetry contests. She also writes fiction and has self published a novel showing how child abuse is handed down from one generation to another.

Printed in the United States
30853LVS00003B/23

9 781418 493417